GW01424415

What
Should Know About...

Praying for
Mission

Every Christian's Responsibility
and Privilege

Margaret Godfree

Sovereign World

Scripture quotations are taken from
the HOLY BIBLE, NEW INTERNATIONAL VERSION.
© Copyright 1973, 1978, 1984 International Bible Society.
Published by Hodder & Stoughton.
Used by permission.

ISBN: 1 85240 295 4

SOVEREIGN WORLD LIMITED
P.O. Box 777, Tonbridge, Kent TN11 0ZS, England.

Typeset and printed in the UK by Sussex Litho Ltd, Chichester, West Sussex.

Acknowledgements

Numerous people have encouraged me in the writing of this little book and I wish to record my gratitude to them for that encouragement.

Special thanks are due to Jean Goodenough of Worldwide Evangelisation Crusade, who not only encouraged me to go on when it had been refused publication, but also spent many hours 'editing' my original, much longer and more rambling manuscript.

It is my prayer that the Lord may use this little effort to encourage others to get involved with praying for world mission. If this happens I shall be more than satisfied.

Contents

1

Why Pray

Untold millions are still untold,
Untold millions are outside the fold.
Who will tell them of Jesus' love
And the heavenly mansions awaiting above?
Jesus died on Calvary to save this world from sin;
Now He calls to you and me to go and bring them in
For many untold millions are still untold.
Untold millions are outside the fold.

This chorus was popular in the missionary meetings I attended as a young Christian in the 1950s and I have often found myself singing it again in recent years as I have become more engaged in intercession for those untold millions. I have also thought of the verse in Romans 10:14-15,

'...how can they believe in the one of whom they have not heard? And how can they hear without someone preaching to them? And how can they preach unless they are sent?' (NIV)

We could add another question, 'How can they be sent, and how can they be effective in their preaching, without adequate prayer input and support?'

Every great missionary endeavour has been backed by believers who prayed and much has been achieved, but after nearly two thousand years of Christianity, there are still whole groups of people who have never heard the truth about Jesus. Some countries used to have thriving churches, but were overwhelmed by Islam or other forces and now few, if any, believers remain. Many people are held so firmly in their religious systems that they do not realise there is any alternative. Millions live in fear of the spiritual and physical consequences of stepping out of line.

Praise God, there are many exciting things happening in missionary terms in different parts of the world, but with every breath you take, you may be sure that someone, somewhere, dies without knowing that Jesus cares about them. Their loved ones go into mourning, grieving helplessly and without hope. Intercessors are still desperately needed to overcome the powers of darkness, and make way for these people to be reached with the gospel. In his letters, Paul repeatedly pleads with us to pray and reminds us of our duty in this respect. All Christians would surely agree that 'the effective, fervent prayer of a righteous person avails much' (James 5:16); but how many really realise the flip side is also true? In the absence of prayer nothing can be achieved!

Any work in the church which is not supported by prayer is likely to be ineffective, whether it is evangelistic effort, administration, youth and Sunday school work or running a jumble sale or coffee morning. People who serve up front, whether in the local church or on the foreign mission field, will only be as effective as the prayer backing they get.

There are many people for whom we should pray, including those in authority in the nation and the Church, church workers, evangelists and missionaries. We should also pray for our families and friends and for those around us who have not yet understood or responded to the gospel message.

Comparatively few are called overseas to share the gospel, but every Christian is called to pray. During a war, not everyone goes to the front line because there is a great deal of vital work to be done in supportive roles such as manning hospitals and producing food and munitions. Without the contribution of these people the war could not be waged, let alone won. It is the same in the spiritual battle: without the prayers of the Church worldwide, many unreached people will remain in the kingdom of darkness.

The command to ask God to send labourers into the harvest field (Matthew 9:38) was given to every Christian, so we all have a duty to help in this way to fulfil Christ's great commission for world evangelisation.

All Christians should be pray-ers. Frequently those who are

unable to minister up front mill along, being led and fed and looked after, not realising that they have the opportunity and responsibility for intercession. A potential army of intercessors sit in church week after week convinced that there is little they can do for the Kingdom of God. Many are loyal church members who really love the Lord and long to serve Him, but they feel they are too ordinary. They have never given prayer much thought and it has never occurred to them that ordinary Christians can serve God through prayer.

Further potential prayer troops could be found among those whose activity level, like mine, is curtailed by sickness or disability. Such people often say, 'All I can do is pray', as though prayer were a second-rate activity for those unable to do anything else. Nothing could be further from the truth.

Others say, 'Yes, we'd like to pray, but we don't know how.' The truth is we need neither special training nor a special calling to pray. The only qualification is that you are a real Christian. You need to be convinced that God's Word is reliable and certain that Jesus is the only way of salvation.

We cannot all go overseas. Perhaps you cannot even go to the local supermarket. But we can all talk to God at home and affect things happening elsewhere, whether down your street or on the other side of the world. Those who do this are just as vital a part of bringing people to Christ as the missionary, evangelist or preacher. Few people will ever know what you are achieving, but God knows.

Ever since my conversion in 1955 at the age of nineteen I have prayed for missionaries. I enjoyed going to missionary prayer meetings and found it a challenge to support individuals and teams working abroad in prayer. I prayed for several friends and contacts around the world and sought to understand what their work involved, praying for protection, health and guidance in their ministry. But my praying rarely got much further than the missionaries and what they were doing. Rarely did I really pray for the people they were trying to reach.

It was only when God called me to Greenland and I began praying for the people of that land prior to going, that I began to feel something of the pain in God's heart over the needs of the lost. I found myself weeping for a people about whom I knew next to nothing.

Years later, when I had to stop work for health reasons, because of a deteriorating back problem, I asked God what He wanted me to do instead. The answer was clear. I was to give more time to intercession for missions. I began to have a deep concern to pray not only for missionaries, but also for the people whom they are seeking to reach with the gospel, and the 'untold millions, still untold' – the unreached people groups of the world.

An elementary lesson? Maybe. But a large percentage of prayer for missions focuses on the missionaries more than the people they serve. Both groups need our prayers.

As I sought to follow the Lord's leading in prayer, He began to teach me how to pray for world missions, especially in those lands from where little or no news filters through and where conventional missionary methods are not possible.

It is my heart's desire to see an army of people pleading on behalf of the 'untold millions' in this world. In the rest of this book I hope to share something of the wonder of prayer – the most fulfilling work there is in the Kingdom of God.

2

General Points

'What is your work for God?' a young man asked me one day.

'Mainly, I pray,' I replied.

'Yes, we all pray, I suppose. But don't you work at all?'

As we talked further he referred to my disability, the long-term effect of an old back injury, and said, 'I don't suppose you can do anything else, can you?'

That week I had spent some hours sorting out the church filing system and had made several visits to an old lady in hospital, and seen her resting in Jesus as she died from cancer. However, these were secondary. My main work for God is prayer – especially for those people who have not yet heard the gospel.

Many people think prayer is easy and can be left to people who cannot do anything else. Some say, 'I'm too busy, I leave the praying to people with time for it.' Others only see prayer as a last resort: 'We've tried everything else, now we can only hope and pray.'

Intercession is not for weaklings, even though many intercessors are physically weak. It is often very hard work and God calls every believer to be involved in it. If we do not do our job effectively, those on the front line will have a harder time, and be less effective. (This does not mean that front-line people can leave all the praying to the intercessors!)

Intercession involves being willing to lay down our own desires and 'rights' in order to be set apart to God. As we move on in intercession, things which are quite permissible now, will come under the searchlight of Heaven, and you will hear the gentle voice of the Spirit saying, 'Let me have that part of your life' or 'that slot of time', or 'that relationship'. But, praise God, we do not need to wait for the process to be completed before we start interceding! As we make time for Him, the Holy Spirit will teach us to pray. He is a good and patient teacher and will not expect a young Christian to begin with a daily four-hour stint of prayer!

The simplest definition of prayer is 'talking with God'. Intercession is simply prayer at a deeper level. 'To intercede' means 'to meet in order to converse', 'to make a petition or plead with a person, for or against others'. Intercession is not a formula or set of rules. It involves pain: learning to know and feel something of the desire of God's heart for a given people or situation and to bring to Him the needs of those people. I personally believe prayer becomes intercession when the burden is so great that you feel yourself to be in the same position as the one for whom you are praying – not that my own prayer times are always like that! Often however, having started by simply talking to God about something, I then begin to share the pain of the people, or feel God's love reaching out to them through me.

Sometimes I feel uplifted and as if I have 'taken off' in prayer. That is great, and it is relatively easy to believe God hears and answers. Just as often, though, prayer is a real slog, with the feeling of just talking into the air with little sense of power. However, faith is not to be governed by what we feel, but by believing God's word and obeying it. Many times I have later been encouraged by hearing how God has answered those hard slog prayers. Remember it is very likely that others are also praying for the same need. God puts all those prayers together. You are not alone, even when on your own, but you are part of a team.

Formal and Informal Prayers

Because of their church background, many Christians find it hard to pray without a framework, and feel most comfortable using set prayers from a book. There is great value in this, and some prayers in the Prayer Book can be used to get you started, so do not hesitate to use them if you find it helpful. Sadly, some Christians, used to 'informal praying', dismiss 'formal' prayers as inferior. Both kinds of prayer can come from the heart and be heard by God. What really matters is whether the prayer is in line with what God wants to do in a given situation.

Having said that, using only pre-written prayers can become

very limiting, and it is good to seek to progress to a deeper friendship with God where two-way conversation becomes more spontaneous and natural.

Essentially we are approaching our Heavenly Father who rejoices to hear even the most faltering words of His children. He does not look for polished, poetic prayers, but for a sincere cry from the heart of someone who loves Him.

Jesus talked about two kinds of prayers: those that are heard and get answers, and those that are not heard and do not get answers. He told us not to use empty repetitions and gave us a valuable pattern prayer. We are well aware that saying set prayers can be little more than empty repetition, but informal prayer can also be empty repetition. I've done it, and heard others doing it. Such prayer is unlikely to achieve much.

The main advantage of 'informal' prayer is that it frees us to pray in all kinds of situations. Paul tells us to 'pray always' (1 Thessalonians 5:17). This does not mean becoming a hermit and cutting ourselves off from everyday life. It means praying even as we go about our daily business. It could be praying over a letter just received from a friend in need, or for disturbing situations as we hear about them on the news. It could be praying for the stranger we pass on the street or for people and needs which pop into our thoughts as we go through the day.

Knowing God's Will in Prayer

When praying, it is important to know God's will. John tells us that if we ask anything according to God's will, He hears us, and if we know that He hears us we know we have the petitions that we asked of Him (1 John 5:14). The question is, how can we know if something is according to God's will or not?

God's Word is very clear about some things. For instance it is His will for people to hear the gospel and have the opportunity to respond in faith and be saved (1 Timothy 2:1-6). So we can pray for those who have not yet heard the gospel, and for those seeking to reach them. Jesus told us to pray to 'the Lord of the harvest…to send workers into his harvest field' (Matthew 9:38 NIV). We can learn to use these scripture truths in prayer that is according to His will as revealed in His Word.

Sometimes we simply assume that we know God's will. For example, because God wants to set captives free, we might pray, 'Lord, release all the Christians from prison in lands where they are persecuted!' But God may actually be using those Christians far more in prison than would be possible if they were to be released. One Christian in the Far East led 188 fellow prisoners to the Lord during his three years' sentence. There are many similar accounts from various countries. As we pray and wait for God's direction He may well lead us so that we come into line with what He really wants. So we pray, 'Lord, You know what is best. Help these prisoners to remain true to you. Strengthen and comfort them, and give them wisdom to say and do the right thing. Use them to speak to their guards and fellow prisoners.'

Similarly, we could be praying for a friend who is in trouble: 'Lord, help Charlie. His business is about to fail and that will mean such hardship for the family.' But, as you continue praying, God shows you that He wants to teach Charlie something through his problems. He may even want Charlie to give up his business and do something quite different in Christian service. God sees things from a higher perspective, and may have a different plan from ours.

When God does not remove problems even when we pray in faith, we need to ask Him to show us how we should be praying. As we become more experienced in prayer, we will learn God's will better. Then we can leave the responsibility of decisions about how and when to answer to Him.

Unanswered Prayer

There are several reasons why God may not answer our prayers in the way we desire, apart from the possibility that He may have a different plan.

James writes in his letter,

'You quarrel and fight. You do not have, because you do not ask God.' (James 4:2 NIV)

We can struggle with some problem, or make all kinds of plans – and still the answer does not come, because we either forgot to pray, or merely asked God to rubber-stamp our own ideas.

Unanswered prayer may be due to sin.

'If I had cherished sin in my heart, the Lord would not have listened...' (Psalm 66:18 NIV)

Sin always hinders our praying. So, when we come to God in prayer, we need to allow Him time to show us if there is any sin which needs dealing with. Confess it, and if you need to put things right with someone else, do so, then ask God to forgive you. (See Matthew 5:23-24.)

Sometimes prayer is unanswered because our motives are wrong. James says that it is possible to ask God for something so that we may spend it on our own pleasures (James 4:3). There is a difference between needs and wants. God will not give His children what we do not need just to gratify our wishes or ambitions. He is unlikely to give you, or your missionary friends, a new car when the old one is in good condition and perfectly adequate for your needs.

However, God is both good and generous, and He often gives us more than our needs, when He knows we can handle it. Then God will want to direct the use of the overflow! It is never given just for our own gratification.

Lack of faith is another reason for unanswered prayers. Faith is not praying in a firm voice and expecting God to back us up. It begins with surrendering to God's sovereignty and trusting Him to know best and to do what is right.

Sometimes, though, our prayers are unanswered even though we prayed in faith according to God's will. This is a real problem for many of God's children today, especially when it comes to praying for healing or for material things. There is a popular teaching that all Christians should always be healed of every sickness and live in prosperity. When this does not happen, they are told it is their own fault because of sin or lack of faith. Then they feel condemned or start digging around looking for hidden sin.

For years I prayed for healing and believed it had to come. In that sense, I did pray 'in faith'. I was also praying in faith for the church and various missionary friends. When the expected answers did not come, I was left clinging to my tattered faith and asking, 'Why, Lord?'

Understanding came slowly as I read the Bible. I saw that faith progresses from asking to listening, and resting in the sovereign power and authority of an Almighty God. True faith persists in prayer, but at the same time submits to God and seeks to learn what He is doing in the situation rather than giving Him orders, or giving up in despairing unbelief (James 1:5-8). Remember this, and keep a balanced view when interceding for someone who is sick or when any prayer appears to go unanswered.

Prayer may also be unanswered because we have not persevered. When Jesus told us to ask, seek and knock (Matthew 7:7) the words used mean that we should ask, and go on asking; seek, and go on seeking; and knock, and go on knocking. Many despair and give up because their prayers are not answered immediately.

Scripture stresses the importance of ongoing prayer and many can testify of the joy when those prayers are finally answered. A missionary prayed for her father's salvation for thirty years before her prayers were answered. Another woman prayed for forty years that God would save her two sons. She died without seeing God answer her prayers, but soon after her death both sons accepted the Lord.

Often, as we go on praying for the same thing for years, the delay teaches us to come closer to God. We learn to find His will in the matter and pray accordingly. The delay brings us closer to God and, as we spend time with the Risen Jesus and the Father, through the work of the Holy Spirit, we are changed into His image. And we can never know the whole story of what is done behind the scenes and in faraway places, because we lined up with Almighty God and prayed for His will to come on a particular spot of earth as it is in heaven.

Some people pray retrospectively. For example, they hear of an evangelistic event that has already taken place, and pray, 'Lord, we pray that they will have had a good time at that event.' It is too late to pray for a good time at an event that has already happened! Even though God is the God of past, present and future, there are no biblical examples of retrospective prayer! Time past is gone and no amount of prayer can change history. However, we can profitably pray that God will bless the follow-up and continue to speak to people who attended the meeting.

Be Specific

When praying it is good to be as specific as possible. I have heard a lot of people pray something like, 'Lord, we pray for Mrs Brown', and I find myself waiting to hear what we are praying for, so I can say 'Amen'. Perhaps God waits as well! Of course He knows that person's needs. But it is a great thrill to pray specifically, and then see how specifically God answers. Bible prayers are usually direct and specific. This does not mean we are allowed to tell God what to do. Rather, we bring specific requests to Him in an attitude of humility and willingness to learn.

Consider a mother praying for her child at school. 'Lord, help David at school...' is a valid prayer, but a bit vague. As the mother seeks God's direction for her prayers, she may find herself praying, 'Lord, please help him when the other boys are so nasty to him and the teacher does not do anything about it.' Later, she may find the Holy Spirit prompting her to pray, 'Lord, help him not to provoke the other boys, and to stand up for himself without being nasty.'

Similarly, 'God bless Mary and John in Africa' is fine, but prayer can be much more meaningful and effective if you find out about their work, needs and the people among whom they minister.

Instead of praying vaguely, 'God bless the vicar...', ask him for prayer requests. He will probably be encouraged that someone cares enough to ask.

3

Getting Started

Setting Aside Time

Effective intercession requires a willingness to be guided by God. However, you do need to have some degree of structure. For most of us, if we wait until we receive some supernatural leading to pray, we will actually do very little praying. Have you ever employed a workman who only worked when he felt like it? Next time I expect you looked for another builder. I suspect that when God wants someone to pray urgently for any situation, He is more likely to prompt those who are already in regular, planned prayer than those who are so 'spiritual' they wait for Him to do it all. So how do we strike a balance between superspiritual prayerlessness and DIY uselessness?

Jesus was the perfect spiritual man, but He was also very practical. He set aside times for prayer, but also prayed at any time when the need arose. It is very important to set aside specific times for prayer. Even though this may not be easy, we can rely on the Lord to help us. Once you have set your time, it may be necessary to let people know you are unavailable at that time, even disconnecting the phone. For many people the best time is first thing in the morning, before everything starts happening. If your special slot gets taken over sometimes, try to arrange an alternative time.

In addition to the set-aside times, we can also pray while doing mundane jobs. During the last two years of my mother's life, I travelled frequently between London and Birmingham in order to help care for her. I found that driving along the M40 could easily be combined with prayer. Of course, I needed to keep alert and pay attention to the road! Closed eyes are not obligatory!

Prayer Topics

If you already have contact with a missionary friend or have an interest in some specific area through your church, that is a good starting point. If there is a group already meeting to pray for that topic, then it is good to join it. News and information are often shared at such meetings, and you could ask to receive prayer letters as well. Then you can go on praying on your own at home as well.

Many mission agencies have prayer groups and also run conferences which can be valuable times of encouragement, gleaning information and meeting some of the missionaries.

'The Field is the World'

This is what Jesus said in Matthew 13:38, but the world is too big for a single individual to pray for in one go! Just as God sends workers to specific areas of His harvest field, so He gives different intercessors different burdens. He will probably assign you an area, but do not become too rigid or limited because He may sometimes give you another assignment for some specific purpose. You will learn to recognise the voice of the Holy Spirit and the way He leads you, which will not necessarily be the same way He leads someone else. God assigns the work and He knows how to ensure that all the needs are covered, but only you can do the work allotted to you. It is unlikely that you will be the only person praying for your area. God knows our weaknesses and failings and also about the need to sleep and do other things. So He calls 'teams' in different parts of the world, in different time zones, so that prayer can go on round the clock. Ask God to show you which part of His work He wants you involved in.

Patrick Johnstone's book Operation World (OM Publishing, 1993) lists all the countries of the world, with a brief outline of the background and needs of each nation, and the missions working there. It also provides addresses of these missions which could be useful in your search for information. Another helpful book is *Praying Through the Window III: The Unreached Peoples* (edited by Patrick Johnstone, John Hanna and Marti Smith and published by YWAM).

Do not get information from too many different sources. Too many prayer requests can be discouraging if we cannot give them proper attention. If we start small, God can enlarge our vision as our capacity grows. If, at any point, you get more letters than you can cope with, ask to be removed from some mailing lists, explaining the reason. Mailing letters costs money and it is not good stewardship to receive letters which you cannot use.

Once you identify an agency working in your area of interest, ask for details and regular prayer information. Some agencies ask for a reference from your vicar or pastor. This is a security measure to protect workers and believers in sensitive areas. Some information could endanger believers' lives if it got into the wrong hands. One worker in a sensitive land sent a detailed letter to her home church, believing they knew how to handle it. Someone pinned it to the notice board in the church porch, where it was seen by an individual who had interests in that land. All the details were fed back to the authorities resulting in trouble for the handful of believers there. There can be a great temptation, if you have news of something that few others know about, to tell all and sundry. You may need to learn to keep your mouth shut for the safety and wellbeing of God's people in difficult lands.

Even when we start small, there are likely to be several different strands to our praying. It is right to pray for our family, friends, church and neighbourhood, and for those who have responsibility for government. Without some organisation, our praying may be haphazard and any prayer letters will be in a constant muddle, so you cannot make full use of them.

There is no sin in being organised, as long as you do not organise God out of the picture! The Holy Spirit must be allowed to change your programme, so it should not be so rigid that you feel condemned every time it gets upset by something else that comes along.

To start with, a simple notebook is probably adequate for listing items for prayer. Alternatively, you could use a diary or loose sheets in a file ruled off with space for each day of the week. My own method is to rule off an A5 sheet into four weekly sections vertically and six daily sections horizontally. (Sunday is for church and refreshing and I keep Saturday for catching up.) I have a list of my prayer areas and people, and I pencil them into this 'diary' to make a possible framework to get started. I use a pencil so it can easily be changed when necessary.

As time goes by, some kind of filing system may be needed for information. I have a floppy plastic A4 file with clear pockets in it for each mission or area I am involved with. As letters come in I read them and mark important topics for prayer and for praise. Having prayed over them they then go in the file, and are taken out and prayed over again as that area comes up on the diary. I pray over the requests mentioned, then try to be open to the Holy Spirit to show me other things and lead me into wider prayer for people and nations.

Snippets of news on the television or radio can also be filed for prayer, as well as maps, pictures and photographs which can be valuable aids to focusing your attention.

As new letters arrive, I normally discard the old ones, unless they contain useful general information, which I keep in a reference file. I make sure that confidential letters from sensitive areas are completely destroyed when I have finished with them.

You will need to develop these things for yourself, in the way most helpful for you. The main thing is to have some order to your praying and a framework in which God can move you around when necessary without leaving you floundering.

Worship First

Before starting to pray it is good to spend some time in reading the Bible and worship, which can be in silence just as much as in singing. Take time to remember who it is to whom you are coming in prayer. As we do this, 'the things of earth will grow strangely dim, in the light of His glory and grace.'* I find it helps to return to worship at intervals during any time of intercession. It is also good, if your prayer time is a bit longer, to return to scriptures which help focus your attention again on Jesus.

Often as I worship or read the Scriptures God shows me how to go on praying. Sometimes in my own devotional reading or Bible study some aspect of truth imprints itself on my mind. Then, when I start praying, I use that scripture to pray for the people of my target area, or for an individual. Later, I may write to the person concerned to share those thoughts.

Then wait quietly asking God to show you how to pray that day. Start by praying for things you know about that concern you but be prepared for God to ask you to pray about other matters as well. Sometimes God will change our prayers completely.

One day, some years ago, I was praying for a situation in Africa, using a world map to help focus my thoughts. However, my eyes kept straying eastwards, away from Africa. I resisted the distraction, but, after a while, it seemed my prayers for Africa had dried up. So I asked God, 'Is there something else you are trying to show me?' It was almost as though He breathed a sigh of relief! At once my eyes were drawn to Mongolia, and the rest of the map went out of focus. I knew virtually nothing about this country which had been Buddhist for centuries and was now under the heel of Communism. As I waited, the clear instruction came into my mind, 'Pray that the people of Mongolia will be able to read the Bible in their own language and that hearts will be opened to receive that word when they read it.' I realised this meant that translators would have to go in and learn the language, getting help from Mongolian speakers. Later there would be all the problems associated with printing and distribution. So I started praying for all this and for the doors to be opened for the gospel to get into Mongolia.

Over the next few months I frequently found myself praying for Mongolia. I prayed that radio ministries would be ready to beam into that land and that teaching materials would be prepared to use in the follow-up of new Christians. I also prayed for God's armies to do battle with the enemy and his dark hosts over Mongolia, opening it up to the gospel. I often felt I was praying for one particular man and his family, though I did not know who they were. At times I sensed a great pressure as I prayed, as though they were in real trouble.

After praying for two or three years, I received a letter telling of a man whom God had called to Mongolia, to study the language and begin translating the Bible. While there, he led a young Mongolian lady to the Lord, and married her. Then he was forced to leave the country. After a time of real trouble, his wife was able to join him in Britain and, together, they went on translating the New Testament into Mongolian. Now it was almost ready for printing. I still get goose bumps of wonder on my neck when I remember that letter coming – just at a time when I sorely needed some encouragement.

Mongolia was still closed, but soon afterwards Communism began to fall apart, and the door opened for this couple to return. A year or so later, I heard of the first ever celebration of Christmas in a Mongolian church.

I do not suppose for one moment that I was the only one praying. (I would find that rather frightening, because I am so fallible and prone to give up.) But the thrill of being a part of something like that far outweighs the cost in terms of lonely hours in prayer, wondering if anything at all is happening.

4

In a Battlefield

Paul tells us in 1 Corinthians 15:20-28 that we are living in a period of spiritual warfare, which will continue until Jesus returns. The term 'spiritual warfare' implies two things: first, that we are engaged in a battle, and, second, that this battle is against a spiritual, rather than a human, enemy.

'*...we do not wrestle against flesh and blood, but against principalities, against powers, against the rulers of the darkness of this age, against spiritual hosts of wickedness in heavenly places.*' (Ephesians 6:12)

Spiritual warfare means working with Jesus to bring His authority to bear in the lives of people, beginning with ourselves, making it possible for the gospel to be proclaimed to all peoples. It includes ensuring, through prayer, that the way is cleared for these people to make their own decision about Jesus Christ. Like the Roman officer who asked Jesus to heal his servant, we need to know that our authority is delegated to us by God and is only effective on behalf of others as we are under Christ's authority. (Read Luke 7:1-10.) As we learn to pray in this authority,

'*...the weapons of our warfare are not carnal but mighty in God for pulling down strongholds, casting down arguments and every high thing that exalts itself against the knowledge of God...*' (2 Corinthians 10:4)

Warfare on a Personal Level

Spiritual warfare involves overcoming temptation and learning to walk with Jesus in obedience, trust and holiness. If our personal warfare is not successful, we cannot expect to be successful on behalf of others. However, this does not mean we have to wait until we are perfect all the time before we start praying for others! Part of our warfare is learning to admit when we have sinned, receiving forgiveness and cleansing, and then going on in our walk with the Lord.

There is no formula for spiritual warfare. In the Old Testament we read of many battles, but God gave different instructions for each one. Jesus also worked in many different ways, following His Father's instructions. To grow in prayer, we need to learn to hear from the Father in just the same way.

Using Scripture in Prayer

The most powerful weapon in intercession is God's word which reveals God's will, enabling us to pray in line with it (see Ephesians 6:17). I sometimes start my intercession by using one of Paul's prayers recorded in his letters, and adapting it to the needs of the person or situation I am praying for. Paul's prayer for the church in Ephesians 3:14-21 could well be used both for the local church and for the Church overseas.

Jesus' own prayers can be used in this way especially those recorded in the final chapters of John's Gospel. In John 17, Jesus prays for His disciples and those who would come afterwards – in other words, the Church. So, when praying for the Church, we can refer to what He said and we will not go far wrong!

God's word can also be used when asking Him to have mercy on the nations. One day, judgement will surely fall on all the nations for their rejection of God's righteous laws, but we can present a case to God, just as Abraham did (Genesis 18 & 19) on behalf of individuals in those nations. We can plead for God's mercy for people who are trapped in belief systems such as Islam, Buddhism or rampant materialism. God will hear our prayers and rescue individuals from destruction just as He did in Abraham's time. In 2 Peter 3:9 we read that it is not the will of God that *'any should perish but that all should come to repentance.'* We can pray with all our hearts that God will move the obstacles and cause the gospel to be preached to all those who have yet to hear.

Many scriptures, such as Psalm 24:1, declare that *'the earth is the Lord's and everything in it'* (NIV). We may refer to the 'Muslim world', the 'world of politics' and so on, but really, by reason of creation, it is God's world, and we should never forget it.

Take care not to misuse scripture in prayer! Some Bible

promises and prophecies refer specifically to Israel and should not be taken out of context.

Confronting the Enemy

The devil has power wherever people, through choice or ignorance, remain under his authority. He has greater power in areas where his authority has not been seriously challenged by prayer and the preaching of the Word of God. Ultimately, of course, his defeat is certain because of the victory won by Jesus at Calvary.

Although we read that Jesus and the early Christians cast out demons from people, I can find no scriptural record of casting spiritual forces out of a nation or other geographical area. However, there is some evidence in Scripture that the ranks of the enemy are well organised and there may be spirit princes in charge of forces in a given area. Daniel 10:13 tells of the prince of the kingdom of Persia, a spiritual being which tried to stop God's messenger getting through. I do believe we can wrestle in prayer, as Abraham did, for a city or nation, asking God to hold back the forces of evil and to reveal His truth and light. We can also declare that the devil was defeated at Calvary, because that is truth.

If a city or a nation abandons God's laws, and sins, then God's judgement will come and He will give them over to the effects of that rebellion. This will, in turn, give place for the devil to increase his hold over them (Romans 1:18-32). In places where there has been little challenge to the forces of darkness, it is reasonable to suppose that the powers of darkness will strengthen their hold over that area. Before we can see a real breakthrough with the gospel, these powers must be challenged and pushed back. But it is not a job to be taken on lightly, or by individual Christians ordering the powers of darkness to depart, even if we do it 'in the name of Jesus'.

I have been in prayer meetings where people have made verbal attacks on the devil and his forces, using the tone one would employ with a naughty child. But evil spirits are not naughty children. They are powerful spirits, at enmity with God and all who belong to Him. Even high-ranking angels of God are careful about how they address the devil (cf. 2 Peter 2:10-11 and Jude 8-9).

Having said that, I have been in other prayer meetings under sound, scriptural leadership, where we have sought God's way to pray for a particular situation and there has come a consensus discernment among the leadership team, which was shared and agreed by the rest of the meeting, that God had given authority to speak words of command to evil forces in that particular situation. We have entered into battle, using God's word directly against the enemy, and experienced the safety which is found close to God's heart. Even in a group we need to be careful it is the Holy Spirit who is guiding us and not our own exuberance. Later, we have heard of real changes taking place as a result of our prayers, clearing the way for God's work to progress.

In all these cases we first drew near to God in worship and obedience, confessing our sins, and waiting for His direction for our intercession.

If you pray alone, it is doubtful whether you should ever take warfare this far. In Greenland a lone missionary climbed a mountain where he began to attack the demonic forces over the town. He became very ill, and had great difficulty getting down the mountain and back to the mission house. There, other missionaries prayed with him and God healed him. Since then, the church, together with teams of intercessors, has done similar things, following times of prayer and fasting and waiting on God, with very positive results.

I once made the same mistake myself. I was asked to baby-sit in a home where the family belonged to Islam. After putting the children to bed, I spent the evening praying. I thought I was doing something wonderful as I 'took authority' over the 'evil spirits of Islam', claiming the family for Christ and pushing back the forces of darkness in Jesus' name. However, during the night I started to have trouble breathing and to feel very ill. As I called out to God for help, I realised I had overstepped the mark by assuming authority which God had not given me. I confessed my presumption and asked for forgiveness and deliverance. The physical symptoms and oppression lifted very quickly, but it took several days to regain my strength.

We need to remember that we are in a battle, and the enemy is not going to give way easily. The greater part of intercessory warfare consists of prayer to God – not direct confrontation with the enemy. We should not neglect this real work of intercession by concentrating on dealing with the devil. It is God Himself who works by His Spirit. When He leads a group to speak His word into a situation, the results are often dramatic.

The Devil's Tactics

In intercession we reach out to God on behalf of others, standing between God and them. If you are serious about intercession, you may be sure that God will help and encourage you. Our battle is not with God or the people we are praying for, but with unseen and extremely malevolent spiritual forces which will do all they can to stop us. Satan hates it when God's people pray, especially for those parts of the world where he has had his own way. Although he tries to stop us, the Bible says, 'He who is in you is greater than he who is in the world' (1 John 4:4). Because the enemy's tactics are often subtle, we need to be particularly alert to them.

Tiredness

The Bible talks of taking up our cross and following Jesus. This can refer to all kinds of things, but one aspect is making the choice between what we want to do and what God wants. Sometimes it is difficult to know whether our problems with prayer have spiritual or natural causes. For example, we may feel tired – so heavy that prayer seems impossible. Natural tiredness may be inevitable sometimes. But it is more likely if we have too many late nights or do not eat the right food.

Chronic illness or pain can make a person tired, making long sessions of prayer impossible. However, it may still be possible to pray briefly, using a prayer list, letters or a map. God hears such prayers which are just as valid as an hour-long prayer stint from someone who is fit and well. Remember how Jesus commended the widow for putting her last pennies in the Temple offering. He did not look at the size of her offering, but saw she had given everything she could.

Prayer Meeting Lethargy

There is another kind of tiredness, though, which I call prayer meeting lethargy. It strikes particularly at times which have been set aside for prayer, either on your own or at a meeting. Suddenly you feel terribly tired. Your eyes are heavy and will not stay open another minute. However, a few minutes after you give up the idea of praying, you take on a new lease of life and can do housework, watch TV, or just about anything! I am still learning to press through this kind of tiredness and pray anyway. Sometimes I recognise the deception when the tiredness lifts. Then I return to prayer.

Whatever the reason, tell God about your tiredness asking Him for the strength to pray and then, even if you feel like a crippled elephant trying to fly, begin to pray. God hears. Many times I have prayed like that, and heard later that just at that time God met a particular need. The crippled elephant never left the runway, but the radio link was still there, and God picked it up and acted on it.

Distractions

Even after getting started in prayer, we may still find ourselves distracted. I suffer from tinnitus and have often answered the door only to find that it was not the bell, but my ears that were ringing! We can also have spiritual tinnitus, where intruding thoughts interfere with our spiritual hearing. We need to cut out as many of these distractions as possible.

Our minds may be filled with the things we see and hear on a daily basis, making it difficult to absorb what God wants to say to us. Clearing our minds from these distractions may involve such things as checking what we watch on television.

We have the authority of Jesus Christ over every attempt of the enemy to distract us from doing God's will. In His name we can learn to resist the devil by using and obeying God's word. But we have to work at it.

If you find a foolproof, scriptural short cut to avoid such problems let me know! But I suspect we are in the same kind of battle that Paul speaks of in 1 Corinthians 9:24-27 – the battle to gain victory over our own bodies and fleshly weaknesses.

5

Praying for the Known

In the time of Isaiah *'truth was nowhere to be found'*, and the prophet declared that the Lord was appalled that there was nobody to intercede (Isaiah 59:15, 16 NIV). If that was the case in Isaiah's day, how much truer it is today among the unreached peoples in religious strongholds such as Islam, Hinduism and Buddhism.

I have a map highlighting those lands where Islam dominates more than 90 per cent of the population. It is an amazingly large area, but very little of the total missionary effort and resources of the Christian world is directed towards these lands. Their peoples are unreached and, in the minds of many, unreachable. Truth, as revealed in God's Word and through His Son, Jesus Christ, is pitifully lacking. In some religions the truth of the gospel has been twisted and changed beyond recognition.

Many agencies have been set up to spread the gospel and do associated work. Some work specifically on translating the Scriptures into languages in which they are not yet available. Others work in partnership with national churches to support them in reaching their own people. Gospel ships travel the world, their crews witnessing and distributing literature. Some agencies are involved in Christian media projects, using literature, radio and television to share the gospel.

In many places, neither missionaries nor Christian literature are allowed. Evangelism is forbidden and converts are liable to persecution and death. In spite of the opposition, expatriate Christians do live and work in some of these lands. Many are involved with humanitarian and secular projects where they can show the love of Jesus and His care in practical ways. Sometimes this leads to opportunities to tell people about Jesus. However, they are closely watched and restricted in meeting together. I salute these people for their stickability in surroundings that are often hostile and where there is little visible evidence of results.

Praying for Missionaries

Most missionaries send newsletters in which they describe their ministry and share their needs to help people pray for them effectively. Some prayer letters give news followed by a list of points for praise and requests for prayer. If the letter does not do this, it is useful to mark these points with a pen as you read it so you can easily identify them when you come to prayer.

It is good to start by praising God for what He is doing in that situation and thanking Him for the workers and the opportunities they have to share the gospel.

Often there will be pointers for ongoing prayer. For example, if a contact has become a Christian, that is a praise item, but you can also pray for his or her spiritual growth, that he or she would get to know God's Word and be able to resist temptation. If the new Christian lives in a country where he or she faces persecution, pray for protection and safety as well as strength to face whatever may come. Pray that the new Christian's family and friends would find Christ as well.

Remember that missionaries are ordinary people who can get lonely and even discouraged. So you can pray for things like companionship with people who speak their own language. They may be in countries where it is hard to get supplies and essential items, or where the cost of living is very high. They may be struggling with a difficult language or culture. The climate may be debilitating, sapping their strength and health. All these things can stimulate our praying. If you read or see on the news that there is some danger or special situation in their country, you can pray about that too.

People Groups

Nearly every country in the world has a mixture of 'people groups'. Each group has its own identity and may be separated from other groups by language or culture. Often there are tensions between them, which can give rise to many problems, even wars and 'ethnic cleansing'. Revelation 7:9 speaks of people from every nation, tribe, people and language standing before

God's throne.

Some people groups cross political boundaries, and this can affect the way we need to pray for them. You might begin by praying for Nigeria, for example. Then God gives you a specific burden for the Fulani tribe. But the Fulani are not confined to Nigeria, but are found in sixteen other African countries as well, not to mention quite a number in France! In some countries they are difficult to reach, but elsewhere they may be fairly accessible. So your praying could include the countries where some Fulani have been reached and have become believers. You could then pray for Fulani Christians to go from these countries to minister to their own people in areas where they are still unreached.

Persecuted Christians

There are Christians in some parts of the world whose faith and way of life are contested by the authorities and by friends and relatives every day. They may be denied the basic essentials of life, tortured, imprisoned and even killed for their faith. Romans 8:38-39, and similar scriptures, can form a valuable guide for your prayers for such people. We can ask God to remind them of these scriptures, and pray that these truths would be very real to them.

Praying for people of other faiths to become Christians is a big responsibility. We are actually praying them into what could be a very difficult and dangerous way of living. We can pray they will experience the truth of Hebrews 11. We should pray that they would be able to withstand all the tricks and attacks of the devil and, even in the face of death, to stand firm in the faith of Christ Jesus (Ephesians 6:13). We can also pray that God would give them His peace.

The peace of God is the peace that keeps God Himself at peace. It kept Him in peace when everything went so horribly 'wrong' in Eden. It kept Him in peace as He planned the way of salvation, and it kept Him as He saw His own Son going to Calvary as part of that plan. At the end of His earthly ministry, Jesus said, *'Peace I leave with you, My peace I give to you'* (John 14:27).

Although we can pray for national and international peace, we should remember that Jesus said that wars would increase as we approach the end time. Real peace between nations will only come when Jesus returns and sets up His Kingdom and rule. Sometimes God allows evil things to happen in order to discipline people and nations. He is not going to bring the kind of peace sought by humanists, politicians and New Agers. If we keep our praying and goals scriptural, then we will not be disappointed!

National Churches

In recent decades we have seen an increasing number of people, from many different cultures and faiths, coming to Britain from all over the world. Many think 'the West' and 'Christianity' are the same thing, and are often appalled at the standards and behaviour of 'Christian' Westerners. We can pray for these people to hear and understand what the Christian message really is. We should also pray for opportunities for real Christians to proclaim the truth about Jesus and His Church in word and in their lives.

Many of those around us have never heard the truth of the gospel in a way which could change their lives. This applies not only to people from overseas, but to many who were born and bred in Britain. The average Briton has little idea of what the Bible teaches or of what Jesus has done for them.

Here is a list of possible subjects to pray for. As you pray, God will guide you as to what He wants you to concentrate on.

Local matters:
- Family and friends
- Workmates and colleagues
- Neighbours and people you meet regularly
- Your local church, your pastor, church leaders
- Sunday school workers and children
- Youth workers and young people
- Other special groups or activities
- Older people in your church and community
- Local government, law and order
- Education and health services.

National matters:
- Your MP and Parliament
- Senior civil servants
- The police
- The armed forces
- The national Church and its leaders.

We are commanded in God's Word to pray for the leaders of our country and also for our church leaders, so these kinds of matters should certainly appear in your prayer diary. When interceding for church leaders, pray that they would be led by God and would stand by the truth of His Word.

6

Praying for the Unknown

Praying over newsletters and information from mission agencies is a vital part of missionary praying, but we need to do more than that if we are to see the darkest areas opened up to the gospel.

Often Christians who reach the boundary of their knowledge of the situation either stop praying or go on to something else. But what about the things that cannot be known? What about the quiet man in your office with problems he feels unable to share? Or the lady down the road, contemplating suicide because of the pressures of domestic problems? Nobody knows about their needs, so nobody prays for them.

What about the missionary who has fallen ill in a remote area without any communications? Or the tribesman travelling in the desert, desperate to know the truth but with no one to guide him? Or the new believer in a land where it is difficult and dangerous to have fellowship with other Christians, and who is in trouble with the authorities because of his/her faith. These people cannot send prayer letters.

Whole areas are still virtually untouched by the gospel. Millions of people live in places where there is little or no missionary or church activity. Are they to be neglected in prayer because nobody knows about them?

No Information
You may feel God is giving you a burden for a particular people group or country, but you have no information and no idea how to pray. Actually you know more than you realise. You know the country is part of God's world and that the people living there are included in His plan to make the gospel known to every person. So you can begin by praying that God will send workers into that

part of His harvest field. Pray they will be fully equipped and have all the back-up they need. Ask God to prepare people's hearts to receive the message and pray for workers to have wisdom and the courage to use the opportunities God gives them.

Pray that the government in that place would not be a hindrance to the work of the gospel and that God would overrule any hostility. Pray that those in authority would themselves find salvation and new life in Jesus.

There! Considering you 'did not know anything about it' that is quite an impressive start! If we fail to find ways of praying for these people, we are failing in the commission Jesus gave us to pray for workers to go into the harvest field.

I have struggled over praying without information, particularly when the Holy Spirit directed my attention to the areas dominated by Islam. But how could I focus my praying on lands and people about whom I knew next to nothing and where I had no contacts. The issue burned in my heart, so I cried long and often to the Lord, 'Teach me to pray.'

As I prayed more, and learned to wait for God's leading, I began to wonder what was happening in the heartlands of Islam. My heart began to ache with longing for the millions living in those lands who had no knowledge of Jesus as Saviour. Although I knew little about Islam, I would often feel such a strong burden that I would cry and cry. Not knowing how to pray specifically, I simply prayed for the people to come to Jesus. I also asked God to teach me how to pray for them.

A turning point came when I read a little book called *The Torn Veil* (Esther Sangster, Marshall Pichering), which tells the story of a disabled Muslim woman who was seeking healing. In the Koran she read accounts of Jesus' miracles and noticed that no such claim was made for Mohammed. God used this to start her searching for Jesus. Then Jesus appeared to her in a vision and healed her, much to the consternation of her family who eventually rejected her. Later Jesus appeared again and told her where she could obtain a Bible and fellowship.

I praised the Lord for this one woman. But what about the millions of others? Then I felt God saying, 'If I could do it once, why not again, multiplied thousands of times, if my people will pray?' So I began to pray that God would turn the eyes of Muslims to parts of the Koran which would make them want to know more about Jesus. I also prayed for Bibles and teachers to become available so they could learn more.

After praying like this for several months, I heard that God was doing this all over the Muslim world. When I found out about the many agencies He had called to this work I was able to receive more information to fuel my praying. Because of the sensitive security situations in many countries news is often limited, so much of my praying is still a matter of listening and going with whatever God shows me.

Praying like this, I have found something of the tremendous joy and excitement of waiting on God and being directed to pray about a situation in some remote part of the world of which I knew nothing at all. Sometimes I have a definite sense of someone in particular need: a Christian in prison who is about to give in and renounce Christ; a family left destitute because they have lost work and status in their community as a result of following Jesus.

God knows who these people are. Even if I get it wrong, it has done no harm. If I am unsure, I pray anyway and leave God to direct the answers to where it is needed. But often I know I am on target because I have such a deep sense of suffering and identification with the people. Later I have sometimes had the awe-inspiring thrill of hearing what God did in that situation. **When we pray like that, God releases His power, preparing the ground for His will to be done in people and nations. Then, suddenly, there is a breakthrough: people start responding, churches are formed, closed lands and hearts are opened, because God's people went on praying even though they did not see anything much happening.**

Reading between the Lines

In some areas a lot of Christian work is going on, but it has to be done with great care because the government or culture is hostile to the gospel. In such places people may pay very dearly for showing an interest in the gospel, let alone converting from their established religion.

Christian workers may suffer intimidation or be expelled from the country. Newsletters must be written with care and readers should be prepared to look for information between the lines. One worker mentioned a man named Paul who had written a second letter to someone called Thess. Alert readers were able to find the verse in 2 Thessalonians which gave very specific information about the worker's problem!

In other cases the letter might refer to something but give little detail. A little thought and prayer, and maybe some research, can often fill in the background situation and lead you to more specific prayer than looks possible at first. If you were in that situation, what would you want people to pray for you?

Third-World Workers

It is very hard for westerners to enter some countries, yet a believer from a neighbouring country could slip in unnoticed and have little difficulty with language and culture. Increasingly, these days, the answer to our prayers for workers may come, not from Britain, but from the Third World, where strong national churches are catching the vision to send their own people as missionaries.

These Third-World workers need our prayers and support. Many come from churches which have plenty of missionary zeal, but very limited resources. We may never meet these missionaries, but we do need to take them on board in our praying. Although links with such workers may be possible through various partnership mission agencies, news is often sporadic and sketchy. Third-World workers may be unable to send letters because of high postage costs, security reasons, or the remoteness of the area where they work.

Our part is to be faithful in prayer. God will surely answer – in His own way and time.

7

Helped by the Holy Spirit

When we reach the boundary of our knowledge, the Holy Spirit can take us through the 'knowledge barrier' into a wider dimension of praying. Paul wrote in 1 Corinthians 14:15 of praying with the understanding, and praying with the Spirit. Both are valid.

According to Paul, the Holy Spirit helps us in our weaknesses, especially where prayer is concerned. When we do not know how to pray, the Spirit Himself makes intercession for us with groanings that cannot be uttered (Romans 8:26).

The many-sided question of spiritual gifts has caused controversy in the Church. If the things I say cause problems for you please do not worry about it. Check what I have written with the Scriptures and ask God to show you if you need to do anything about it. Let Him lead you in His way for you.

Praying in the Spirit is not some superhuman phenomenon, out of the reach of ordinary people. In a very real sense, all effective praying is 'in the Spirit' since it is only by the Holy Spirit that we have access to God anyway.

Personally, although I often pray in tongues, I do not believe that speaking in tongues is the primary and only evidence of being filled with the Holy Spirit or of a person's level of spirituality. I have known many who speak in tongues whose lives do not measure up to the standard of Scripture, and others who do not speak in tongues, but whose spirituality is beyond question.

I have learned in over forty years as a Christian that 'different' does not always equal 'wrong'. I have seen, and suffered from, very harmful excesses, but I have also learned to value the real work of the Holy Spirit in my life, and also in the church, through the properly monitored manifestation of spiritual gifts.

In 1 Corinthians 14:1-19, it seems that when Paul speaks of

praying in the Spirit, he is linking it, at least in part, with praying in tongues. It is true that spiritual gifts have often been misused, and that is a serious matter which some parts of the Church need to examine carefully. But the solution is to use the gifts according to scriptural principles, not to abandon their use altogether.

My experience of speaking in tongues has been a tremendous source of blessing and help in fellowship with God, in praise, worship and prayer, both on my own and with others, but only if I know it will not give offence to others present.

Usually, I cannot claim to recognise a particular language when I speak in tongues, though, on one occasion when I was working in Denmark, I was sure God had given me a prophetic word for the church. Although I was not at all sure of my ability to give it in Danish, I felt strongly challenged to start speaking and trust God with the outcome. I found myself using words I had never consciously heard before. Afterwards, people told me I had used a poetic style of Danish rather like our King James Version and many in the church were encouraged by the word from God.

I do know that when praying in tongues I often seem to use different 'languages' for different parts of the world. I sometimes wonder whether God gives us languages and dialects which are no longer used. This is pure speculation, of course! I once heard of an Eskimo, who spoke only his own Inuit language, praising God in old-style English when he was filled with the Holy Spirit.

In worship there often comes a point when I find that English simply does not have enough words to express what my heart wants to say to God. Similarly, in prayer, there comes a point when I know I should pray some more, and the burden is almost a physical pain, but words no longer express that burden. Then I simply let the Holy Spirit take over. As He gives me the language there is a great release within. Prayer rises to a higher level as though I have grown wings and am soaring up to God where I can see things from His viewpoint. Situations that were muddy become clear and this clearer view enables me to pray in English again, but with greater understanding.

I know people who have this sort of experience without actually speaking in tongues. That is fine. I have no wish to say that everyone must do it the way I do!

Unutterable Groanings

Sometimes when we are praying our burden is so deep and painful it cannot be expressed even in tongues. Perhaps we are deeply concerned for a son who is making a mess of his life, or a close friend who is seriously ill. Or it may be the desperate plight of the poor and homeless on the streets of our town, or the need of those who are dying without Christ, never having had the chance to hear the gospel. In such situations, you can call on the Lord with the groaning of your heart. I have often just lifted a situation up to God, and simply pleaded, 'Jesus, you know! Undertake, please...'

At times the burden may be so great that deep emotions are stirred and tears flow. Do not be afraid of expressing yourself in this way, but crying has no merit of its own, so do not try to make yourself cry! I have met people who have done this! God created your emotions, and He will use them to release the cry of your heart when words are not enough.

If you do not experience this when you pray, you are not inferior to someone who does. The important thing is not whether you groan, cry, or use tongues when you pray. The important thing is that you pray from your heart, and that you are always open for the Lord to teach you more.

Besides the gift of tongues, other spiritual gifts are mentioned in the Bible, one of which is the word of knowledge mentioned in 1 Corinthians 12:8. This is a revelation from God, who knows everything, of a little bit of His knowledge about a given need or situation. For instance, when we are praying for something about which we know little, God may reveal something to us to help our praying. He may even show us a situation about which we know nothing at all so that we can pray about it.

A 'word of knowledge' is often accompanied by 'a word of wisdom', so that we know what to do with it! These words are given for specific reasons, and should not be shared with anyone else unless the Lord shows you that you should do so.

Once I was praying for a man in great need. God showed me something about him which was very specific and relevant to his problem. Getting words of knowledge was a bit new to me, and I had to decide whether or not to speak to him about it. Realising I might cause unnecessary hurt by speaking about it, I went to my pastor for advice. I discovered he was actually praying with this man and counselling him. He confirmed that the word of knowledge was on the right lines and suggested how I should pray for the situation, but advised me not to say anything about it. This advice proved to be God's word of wisdom for me.

I went on praying without saying anything. In a meeting a few weeks later, the man testified how God had wonderfully met his need on the issue for which I had been praying. He still does not know of my prayers for him at that time. We are told to pray to the Father in secret, and He who sees in secret will reward us (Matthew 6:6).

Knowledge can be revealed in various ways. It can come through a dream or a mind picture, which some call visions, or a strong and persistent impression or unexpected thought about something or someone.

I vividly recall the first time I was aware of this kind of leading in prayer. During the early days of the war in Vietnam I was in a prayer meeting when I began to get a picture in my mind of a house made of wood and grass and surrounded by tropical trees. A man and woman and a little girl with very fair hair were barricaded inside the house which was then set alight.

I had a terrible sense of urgency. Unsure what to do, I quietly shared the vision with the pastor who felt God was showing us something about which we should pray. He asked if I had any idea who the people were or where it was happening. I had a distinct impression that it was in Vietnam. There were still missionaries in South Vietnam, and I had a friend working there, but she did not fit this picture at all. The pastor shared the vision with the others and we began to pray for the deliverance of this little family. Several people cried out to God together as the urgency of the situation gripped us. After about an hour there was a general agreement that we had prayed through and we had a time of rejoicing. After the meeting, I went home thinking, 'What an odd thing to happen!' Had I just been imagining it all?

A few weeks later my friend in Vietnam wrote to me. She said she would be coming home for an early furlough because a nurse was required to accompany a family who had some injuries which needed treating at home. The parents and their little girl had been barricaded into their house which had then been set alight! God had alerted local believers who had rescued them.

Later I met the family concerned and we compared notes. I was awe-struck to discover how the timing of our prayer meeting fitted in with the time they were in so much danger.

Another 'vision' came when I was cooking dinner for myself and a friend in Denmark. I had an impression of a terrific storm at sea, and a map of the Indian Ocean where a big, black, swirling mass was moving towards Bangladesh. A few weeks previously a storm had caused great damage in that land. I felt a great surge of compassion which led me to abandon the cooking and call my friend so we could pray together. We called on God to be merciful to the people of Bangladesh. When we felt the burden lift, we returned to our dinner. Later we heard on the BBC World Service that a storm, which had been heading for Bangladesh, had inexplicably turned and was blowing itself out at sea!

We may 'see' things in 'visions' which appear to contradict our own experience and knowledge. Praying one day for Greenland, and especially for the Christians in the capital, Nuuk, I had the impression I was walking round the town with missionaries and other Christians, praying outside various buildings. I knew some of the buildings, which prompted me to pray for the authorities, government departments, the hospital and so on. I seemed to see other buildings which I did not recognise, but prayed as I felt the Holy Spirit was leading me, sometimes in tongues. Then it seemed we were walking through a tunnel in the mountain and out the other side into a new town, where we continued praying. I was sure this was not right, because I had lived in Nuuk, and knew there was no tunnel through the mountain! I wondered if it represented a dark time ahead, and that they would pray through to victory.

I wrote to my Danish friends in Nuuk telling them about the vision. They phoned in some excitement. My letter had arrived just at the time when they were planning a prayer walk round the town. The vision confirmed that they were to do it, and even gave them some leads as to how to pray. Imagine my surprise and awe when they told me that a tunnel had been blasted through the mountain and the town extended on the other side. They had actually been praying about extending the work and taking the prayer march through the tunnel!

These are dramatic examples. It is not by any means always like that! About 80 per cent of my praying is the ordinary, hard work kind, where I pray through information and needs that I know about, or cry out to God for His mercy on a particular people group. Often I have little idea what happens as a result. That is left in God's hands. But there is a great joy in getting a newsletter telling how God has undertaken in a situation for which I have been praying.

The rewards of intercession are many: the delight of doing God's will, the thrill of answered prayer, and sharing the joy in heaven when another person puts his or her trust in Jesus.

Appendix
Suggested Prayer Diary for Your Missionary

The following is taken, with permission and a few minor adjustments, from the prayer letter of a friend working in a foreign country.

Sunday – Spiritual Life

'When your words came, I ate them; they were my joy and my heart's delight, for I bear your name, O Lord God Almighty.' (Jeremiah 15:16 NIV)

Contrary to popular belief missionaries are not spiritual giants. They are subject to the same doubts, temptations and struggles that their counterparts at home face. But the crucible of the mission field may make these difficulties even more pronounced. Pray to the Author of our Faith for:

- consistent times of prayer and learning from Scripture;
- meaningful worship and fellowship time;
- love, joy, peace, patience, kindness, goodness, gentleness, faithfulness, self-control;
- victory over Satan;
- commitment to the work.

Monday – Ministry

'Those who are wise will shine like the brightness of the heavens, and those who lead many to righteousness, like the stars for ever and ever.' (Daniel 12:3 NIV)

God does not call missionaries to foreign lands simply to subsist, raise a family, and become multilingual. They have been sent to minister. But the technicalities of living overseas often keep missionaries from fulfilling their purposes. Beseech the King of Kings for:

- a work of the Holy Spirit in the hearts of the nationals;
- boldness;
- the projects with which they are involved;

- the people for whom prayer is requested;
- wisdom in the use of time, resources and energy.

Tuesday – Family

'Therefore, since we are surrounded by such a great cloud of witnesses, let us throw off everything that hinders and the sin that so easily entangles, and let us run with perseverance the race marked out for us. Let us fix our eyes on Jesus, the author and perfecter of our faith...' (Hebrews 12:1-2 NIV)

Many effective missionaries have been lost to the field due to family complications. Whether it is inadequate schooling for their children, elderly parents who need care at home or a family whose behaviour falls short of Christlikeness, Satan often uses these kinds of problems to hinder effective ministry. Pray to your Heavenly Father for:
- strong marital relationships;
- support from family at home;
- enabling to be an example to the people they live among.

Wednesday – Relationships with Fellow Workers

'Do not get drunk on wine which leads to debauchery. Instead, be filled with the Spirit. Speak to one another with psalms, hymns and spiritual songs. Sing and make music in your heart to the Lord, always giving thanks to God the Father for everything in the name of our Lord Jesus Christ. Submit to one another out of reverence for Christ.' (Ephesians 5:18-21 NIV)

The image of a lone missionary settling in a remote village, struggling to learn an unwritten language, introducing the entire population to Christ, returning to churches at home to report on progress, may be attractive but is not necessarily accurate. Your missionary may well be working as part of a team made up of nationals and other missionary organisations, as well as prayer partners. Working with a team is never easy, even less so when different cultures are involved. Ask the Mighty Counsellor for:
- a spirit of co-operation on the team;
- eagerness to submit to and learn from each other;

- lack of friction;
- willingness to confront lovingly;
- accountability.

Thursday – Place of Service

'After this I looked and there before me was a great multitude that no-one could count, from every nation, tribe, people and language, standing before the throne and in front of the Lamb. They were wearing white robes and were holding palm branches in their hands. And they cried in a loud voice, "Salvation belongs to our God, who sits on the throne, and to the Lamb."' (Revelation 7:9-10 NIV)

Knowing about the climate, history, religion, and government where your missionary works will aid you in praying more intelligently. Perhaps visas are hard or impossible to get so your missionary may need to move to another country. Pray for:
- the political and economic situation;
- growth of the national Church in the region (if there is one);
- safety for Christian workers;
- perseverance as they train and work;
- clear guidance each step of the way as they move into the work to which God has called them.

Friday – Ability to Communicate

'Preach the Word; be prepared in season and out of season; correct, rebuke, and encourage – with great patience and careful instruction.' (2 Timothy 4:2 NIV)

Your missionary needs to learn the language of the people they will be reaching, in order to communicate God's love in the language of their hearts, in a culture where things are often drastically different from back home. Not only must they learn the language but they must also learn the culture. Pray for:
- diligence in language study;
- national contacts from whom to learn the language and culture;

- willingness to 'hit the streets' and practise regardless of how weak their linguistic abilities may seem;
- communication with family, supporters and team-mates;
- ability to minister to others in a new language.

Saturday – Physical Needs

'And my God will meet all your needs according to His riches in Christ Jesus.' (Philippians 4:19 NIV)

Financial support, good health, equipment, transportation, adequate housing, and safety in sometimes dangerous situations... The physical needs of your missionary are great! But so is our Lord's ability to provide! As you receive newsletters you will know what to pray for specifically. But here are some general suggestions to help you get started. Pray to the Great Provider for:

- health and safety;
- deliverance from depression, loneliness or anxiety;
- housing, schooling and transportation needs.

****

If you have been challenged by this book and need help in following it through, please write to me and I will do my best to help.

Miss Margaret Godfree

11 Pilgrim Gardens, Grocot Road, Evington, Leicester, LE5 6AL.